D0991534

To Zhu Xiao-Mei, the virtuoso pianist who, in April 2007, told me her story and encouraged me to interpret it with 'imagination' for the children of today.
A.L.

To Catherine and André, with all my love. And thanks to Isabelle for the old Chinese papers.
B.

HISTORICAL NOTE FOR PARENTS, TEACHERS AND OLDER READERS

The Cultural Revolution was started by Chinese leader Mao Tsetung in 1966 to make China's people follow his idea of the way they should live. For about 10 years, he encouraged everyone to carry and quote from a 'Little Red Book' of his sayings and commands. Young people left school and became Red Guards, roaming the country to search for and destroy the 'four olds'—old customs, old culture, old habits and old ideas. Temples and religious statues were torn down, books and paintings burned, schools and universities closed.

People who had lived overseas, had studied at university, owned houses or land, or created Western-influenced art, literature or music were beaten, sometimes even killed—or, like the little girl in this book, they were sent to the countryside to work with the peasants.

We have prepared special notes to help you understand the historical period in which this extraordinary book is set, and the human rights issues it raises. Visit our website at **www.wilkinsfarago.com.au** or email sales@wilkinsfarago.com.au to receive your free copy.

First published in Australia and New Zealand in 2009 by
Wilkins Farago Pty Ltd, PO Box 78, Albert Park, Victoria 3206, Australia
Reprinted 2011
Teachers' notes and other downloads: **www.wilkinsfarago.com.au**

© Éditions du Sorbier, 2008
Calligraphy on page 31 by Dr Pei-Yuan Han
Graphic design: francis m
English translation: Justine Werner

National Library of Australia Cataloguing-in-Publication entry
Author: Leblanc, Andre, 1940-
Title: The red piano / Andre Leblanc ; illustrator Barroux.
ISBN: 9780980607017 (hbk.)
Target Audience: For children.
Subjects: Zhu, Xiao-Mei.
Pianists--China--Biography--Juvenile literature.
Dewey Number: 786.209

This book is copyright. Apart from any fair dealing for the purposes of private study, research, criticism or review, as permitted under the Australian Copyright Act, no part may be reproduced by any means without written permission from the publisher.

Printed in Singapore by Toppan Security Printing Pte. Ltd.

Distributed by the Scribo Group (Australia) and Addenda Publishing (New Zealand)

ANDRÉ LEBLANC
ILLUSTRATED BY BARROUX

The red
piano

China, 1975, one April evening.

*For seven years now, educated young people have been going to re-education camps, occasionally with
enthusiasm but more often than not under duress. Their mission: to eradicate elitism through manual labour
alongside poor farmers and by studying Chairman Mao's political works.*

'Revolution is not a dinner party!'

WILKINSfarago

South Huntington Pub. Lib.
145 Pidgeon Hill Rd.
Huntington Sta., N.Y. 11746

Zhangjiake Camp 46-19 on China's border with Inner Mongolia is blighted by an eerie moonlight.

In the hut, the cramped rooms reek of warm sweat, the foul smell of extinguished coal fires and packed earth. Crammed together, the comrades are already sleeping on the bare ground. Taking small, careful steps, the young girl leaves the communal house.

Outside, the wind is lashing.

There is supposed to be a strict curfew, but it has been a long time since the Committee posted guards to keep watch. All she has to do is jump the latrine wall and follow the tree-lined path. At the end of the path, on the village's edge, she can already make out the house of Mother Han, her accomplice.

An upright piano occupies the store room, its keyboard yellow in the lamplight.

A low chair is drawn up and frozen hands raised. Then, a pause. Thoughts go back to a previous life, to the whisper of her first music teacher:

'You need to warm up your hands with a Bach Prelude, little one, rather than hammering at the keyboard like a maniac!'

She leans forward, her frail body lost in her blue jacket, her plaits brushing against the keys and, without waiting any longer, she launches into her Prelude. Warmth returns ...

The music rises, free yet encased by the thick walls. Tonight marks the end of her fifth year in exile. Like thousands of others, her father, mother and four sisters have been dispatched to other camps. Pianos are criminal. Pianists are criminals. Schools are closed down. The Communist Party is re-educating everyone.

From sunrise to sunset, she has to learn a new way of life: how to plant rice, collect vegetables, pick fruit and chop wood in her working group. They call it 'learning through labour and self-criticism'. The Great Chinese Cultural Revolution continues.

Her fingers fly across the keyboard. The day's woes are
forgotten, along with the late hour, the tiredness and the
danger. Concentrating, determined, she senses the keys.
Right hand, left hand: practising arpeggios, cadences and
counterpoint ...
There's a fleeting half-smile ...

Yesterday, an astounded guard caught her red-handed.
She pretended she was rehearsing a revolutionary opera
composed by Chairman Mao's wife ... He went away ...
'Long live Chairman Mao!'

Bringing a piano all the way here—what a crazy venture!
Three years ago, her sick mother was evacuated to Beijing.
The young pianist, deprived of an instrument, hatched
a plan, sent secret messages, and relentlessly tried to
persuade her ... Her mother ended up giving in: she'd find
her a piano.

The piano traveled in a coal wagon aboard the train bringing supplies to the camp. Three weeks of travelling, a few strings broken. All you could hear of the high notes was the 'doink' of the hammers, but the low notes held up better: resonant, deep ...

A piano at Zhangjiake Camp 46-19: a miracle!

Tonight she is transported back to her childhood and the muffled noise of the city. She was her mother's great hope. Gifted at the piano. Plenty of good luck and ten long hours of music practice every day. Music at mealtimes, music before going to sleep. Six years at the music school for gifted children. Concerts on Beijing radio.

She almost came to hate the piano! But tonight, at her run-down instrument, she savours a deep-rooted happiness ten times greater than ever before!

For several years now, pages from Bach's *The Well-Tempered Clavier* have been passed round the camp, from hand to hand. The father of a friend sends parcels. Several sheets are hidden in each package. If there is an inspection, they are confiscated; and she has to hope for another package.

She decides to make her own music book and starts copying out the *Clavier* into slim, handmade notebooks. Thin sheets of fragile, reused paper. The more she writes, the smaller her writing becomes. She's scared of running out of space.

During the self-criticism classes, three hours a day after work, she uses her *Little Red Book* to hide her project. She copies the staves, the notes, each part beneath her tunic. For weeks, she applies herself steadily, page after page. Now she has several little notebooks hidden away.

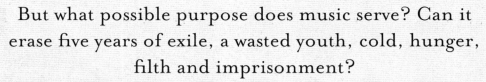

But what possible purpose does music serve? Can it erase five years of exile, a wasted youth, cold, hunger, filth and imprisonment?

For three years, every evening, for two hours after the work in the fields and the self-criticism class, her hands rediscover the grumbling old piano.

Playing for the love of music. It's as simple as that!

An echo of the music inside us all, which, little by
little, has brought some humanity into her life and
into a system that has none.
It's a strength. A madness, too!

Last month, the Philadelphia Orchestra was in Beijing.
Going back down into the valley, slipping onto a train.
Two hundred kilometres of risks, from the Mongolian
border to the capital.

Music, happiness ... and a hint of freedom!

Tonight, in the grip of her music and her memories,
the young pianist doesn't hear Mother Han's muffled
cry. Nor does she sense the presence of intruders.
Looking down from her left hand as it gallops towards
the lowest notes, she suddenly glimpses two pairs
of boots and green uniforms. Her heart stops. Her
fingers freeze in mid-air.

The head of the camp and his deputy are standing in
the doorway. Her last notes hang briefly in the air.
There is a long silence.

All of a sudden she jumps up. Her chair falls over.
With her head bowed, she rushes outside.

The Deputy shouts after her, 'Your music is not worth
a dog's fart!'

Running like mad towards the huts, she can no longer
hear …

In the morning, in front of the assembled village, she and her accomplice are denounced, lectured and insulted. The Deputy mockingly hangs signs around their necks stating their offence.

The piano is dragged onto the square and brutally smashed into firewood. The strings are rolled onto spools and used to tie up the bundles of firewood. Each family receives their share. Except the educated families, of course.

The ceremony ends. Everybody heads to the fields singing patriotic songs.

Mother Han is driven out of the village.

The young pianist is kept at Zhangjiake 46-19 by the guards. Her re-education is intensified. Her stay is extended. Collecting human compost from the latrines and transporting it to the fields, to fertilise the soil: this is what happens to a rebellious artist.

And the music in her heart subsides.

A year goes by.

September 1976. Chairman Mao is dead. Zhangjiake
Camp 46-19 starts to empty.

One evening, she is called in front of the Committee.
She is worried.

In the cold, grey room, beneath a glaring portrait of
Mao, the head of the camp tells her that she's going
back to Beijing. She leaves at dawn. She is the last to
leave Zhangjiake 46-19 re-education camp.